Dialectical Behavior Therapy for Addiction

The Easy Self - Help Guide - Simple Steps to Conquering Addictions to Porn - Eating Disorders - Substance Abuse - Alcohol and Drugs - Online Gambling

liable for any hardship or damages that may befall them after undertaking information described herein. Additionally, the information in the following pages is intended only for informational purposes and should thus be thought of as universal. As befitting its nature, it is presented without assurance regarding its prolonged validity or interim quality. Trademarks that are mentioned are done without written consent and can in no way be considered an endorsement from the trademark holder.

Table of Contents

Chapter 2: Overcoming Addictions to Porn via Dialectical Behavior Therapy

Understanding Why Porn is an Issue
Qualifying one as an Addict of Porn
Causes of Addiction to Porn
Impact of Porn Addiction
Dialectical Behavior Therapy as a Remedy for Porn Addiction

Understanding Dialectical Behavior Therapy

Handling Porn Addict using the Modules of Dialectical Behavior Therapy

I.   Core Mindfulness Module
II.   Emotion Regulation Module
III. Distress Tolerance Module
IV.   Interpersonal Effectiveness Module

Ways of Implementing Dialectical Behavior Therapy to Address Porn Addiction

I.   Cognitive-Based Approach
II.   Collaborative Approach
III. Support-driven Approach

Developing Objectives using Dialectical Behavior Therapy to Overcome Porn Addiction
Implementing Dialectical Behavior Therapy Programs
Qualification of Dialectical Behavior Therapy
Summary

Chapter 3: Employing Dialectical Behavior Therapy to Overcome Online Gambling Addiction

Understanding what Online Gambling Addiction is
Why Online Gambling Worsens Addiction
Dialectical Behavior Therapy to Overcome Online Gambling

Chapter 4: Employing Dialectical Behavior Therapy to Overcome Food Addiction

Conclusion

Description

Introduction

Addiction is one of the most prevalent forms of disease in the current generation. It is a persistent kind of disease shown by wanting to use drugs; it is difficult to manage and control even though it has adverse and harmful results. Most people use drugs voluntary for healing purposes but consistent substance use leads to brain damage or a change in the proper functionality of the brain. This is due to the fact that the person has no self- control to the drug and is also unable to resist the drug. We have various forms of addiction today such as:

- Addiction to porn

- Addiction to drugs and alcohol

- Addiction to online gambling

- Addiction to food

This book discusses the different forms of addiction and their symptoms, and factors that lead to addiction. Most of addicts try alternate ways to stop this adverse behavior but find it difficult stopping long-term. The book discusses how addicts of various types can be assisted through Dialectical Behavior Therapy. This is a kind of treatment that the addict undergoes to help them manage impulsive feelings and learn to accommodate stress and develop desired interpersonal skills. Dialectical Behavior Therapy uses modules in overcoming various addictions and it can be implemented to address substance abuse.

Chapter 1: Applying Dialectical Behavior Therapy on Alcohol and Drugs Addiction

The chronic use of alcohol and drugs to the level that is higher than the daily allowed dosage and causes withdrawal symptoms is known as alcohol and drugs addiction. High dependence on alcohol is referred to as alcoholism and it predisposes an individual to co-occurring conditions like substance abuse. Sometimes, individuals develop an addiction to both alcohol and drugs with devastating consequences. Abusing both alcohol and drugs can adversely affect your behavioral, physical, and mental health leading to complications. Persons who abuse alcohol have a high likelihood of engaging in the use of hard drugs such as heroin and marijuana. The unholy combination of drug use and alcoholism can cause devastating health complications within a short period of time. For this reason, alcohol and drug addiction is a major issue and this chapter will tackle the definition, effects, and how to address alcohol and drug addiction using dialectical behavior therapy.

Detecting Alcohol and Drug Addiction

Not every symptom of abuse of alcohol or drug is easily detectable. Some individuals may try to mask their drug and alcohol use making it difficult to diagnose their addiction problem. The reason for this hideous behavior is because of the negative connotations and stigma linked to alcohol and drug abuse. Family members and friends can only get involved if they can read the signs that the person is abusing alcohol or drugs. Signs that you might be on the path of abusing alcohol include being uneasy with those condemning drug use or alcohol. If at one point or several times you have urged yourself that you need to cut down on your drinking or use of drugs, then you are becoming aware that you need help. The other sign that you are probably abusing alcohol or drugs is when you start feeling guilty over your consumption of alcohol or drugs. Individuals who exhibit addiction to drugs or alcohol crave for these substances periodically throughout the day. Symptoms of drug use or alcohol consumption may include having challenges executing routine tasks because of taking or not taking drugs or alcohol.

Alcohol addiction involves the inability to manage drinking habits, commonly known as alcohol use disorder. This occurs when a person becomes psychologically or physically dependent on alcohol. Alcohol is an addictive substance. Everyone who takes alcohol will not become addicted. Nonetheless, some people can be more prone to addiction compared to others. Alcohol abuse and addiction are not the same. Thus, it is important to comprehend the meaning of alcohol addiction. Being an alcohol addict refers to as overdependence on alcohol that does not stop despite adverse consequences. People that suffer from alcohol addiction become physically dependent on it and experience mild withdrawal symptoms. Consumers of too much alcohol are not necessarily addicted to alcohol. These are just heavy consumers who continue consumption despite consequences.

Symptoms of Alcohol Addiction

Addicts of alcohol do not often show the same symptoms. Individual symptoms depend on a number of reasons,e.g an individual's medical and background history.

Indicators showing one is an alcohol addict

- Not being able to stop drinking.

- Neglecting family/personal responsibilities.

- Driving while drunk.

- Inability to control alcohol consumption.

- Drop in academic and professional performance..

- Internal quarrels with people you love.

- Cravings and preoccupation with drinking

- Inability to control drinking.

Alcohol Addiction and its Effects

Effects of alcohol abuse differ with individuals but can touch on every aspect of one's life. Too much use of alcohol can affect your career, health, and family.

Short-Term Effects

This depends on the amount of alcohol consumed and the body state of a person.

These include:

- Anemia

- Upset stomach

- Loss of memory

- Drowsiness

- Diarrhea

- Coma

- Feeling dizzy always

- Breathing difficulties

- Poor vision and hearing

- Impaired judgment

- A decline in perception and coordination

- Unconsciousness

Long-Term Effects

These also depend on the amount of alcohol consumed by an individual and also his/ her body state, it can cause:

- Vomiting
- Diarrhea
- Feeling dizzy
- Poor speech (stammering)
- Frequent stomach aches
- Difficulty in breathing
- Poor in decision making
- Poor vision and hearing.
- Frequent headache
- Decreased perception and coordination
- Loss of blood in the body due to lack of enough red blood cells
- Loss of memory within a short period of time

Addiction to Drugs

This is also known as substance use disorder. It affects a person's behavior and brain that causes him/her the inability to control its use or proper functionality. One chooses to consume a drug because it makes them feel good in a certain way. It may seem easy to control depending on how much and how often one uses it. But with time, it changes their behavior and functionality of the brain. Physical changes last for a long period of time which makes them lose self-control.

Symptoms of Drug Addiction

Symptoms of drug addiction include:

- Experiencing withdrawal symptoms when trying to stop consuming the drug.

- Feeling that one needs to use the drug often

- Always thinking about the drug and how you will get it and nothing else

- The desire to take much of the drug often over time

- Consuming larger amounts of the drug for a long period of time

- Overspending money on the drug, even when you lack the money to buy it

- Spending less on your recreational and social activities

- Always have the urge to use the drug though it has already caused you physical repercussions

- Improper behavior such as stealing so as to get the drug

- Driving when you are under the influence of the drug

- Using most of your time to obtain the drug rather than using your time in a more productive way

- Failed attempts to stop using the drug

- Having withdrawal symptoms in a bid to stop the behavior

Consequences of Drug Addiction

Consequences of drug addiction can be felt by the addict psychologically or physically.

Psychological Effects

Psychological effects are caused by the factors that made the user an addict to drugs, also the changes that took place in the brain when the person became an addict. Originally, a lot of people used drugs to keep up with pain or stress.

Psychological effects include:

1. Psychological endurance to the substance affects craving to consume in large amounts

2. Anxiety, depression, paranoia

3. The decline in relaxation of day-to-day life

4. Mental illness

5. Confusion

6. Violence

7. Appetite in engaging in awkward behavior

8. Craving

Physical Effects

These consequences are different depending on the type of drug but are normally observed in all organs of the human body. Most of the time they occur in the brain. It transforms the functionality of the brain's core function and affects how the body system perceives pleasure.

Physical effects of drug addiction include:

- Hepatitis, contraction of HIV

- Heart attack and heart problems

- Lung cancer

- Pain in the Abdomen

- Constipation

- Diarrhea

- Vomiting

- Liver damage

- Failure of the kidney

- Complications of the Brain

- Stroke

- Loss of appetite

- High body temperature

Types of Addictive Drugs

Depressants

➤ Also known as downers, they reduce the activity of the brain to keep the body in an extreme relaxing mood. It becomes harmful if it is taken more as per the dose to reach the maximum state, or mix with other substances such as alcohol to enhance their effects.

Mostly abused depressants include:

- Sedative-hypnotic

- GHB

- Benzodiazepines

- Barbiturates

When abused, depressants may slow down the person's breathing rate such that it can cause death.

Symptoms of Addiction to Depressants:

Persons are fast to acquire a state to cope with the depressants when used for a long period. Suddenly stopping its use may lead to severe withdrawal symptoms.

Heroin

➢ Also known as diamorphine illegal opioid synthesized from morphine.

➢ Used as a recreational drug for euphoric effects. Physical overdependence commonly results in traumatic withdrawal symptoms experienced by users. These poses public health threats; shared needles and unhygienic behavior leaves the users at a greater risk of contracting HIV or AIDS and Hepatitis.

Hallucinogens

Synthetically obtained, they cause sensory disorders. Prolonged use may lead to users experiencing substantial changes in thoughts, emotion, and consciousness relapse long after using drugs.

Mostly used hallucinogens include:

- LSD

- Ketamine

- Psilocybin

- Ecstasy

- Spice

- Mescaline

Symptoms of Addiction to Hallucinogen:

Consequences may begin within ninety minutes of its consumption. It takes up to 12 hours. Most signs of a hallucinogen addiction include:

- A rise in body temperature

- High blood pressure

- Psychosis

- Paranoia

- Over sweating

- Dry mouth

- Spiritual experience

Factors Leading to Drug Addiction

1) Trauma

Events leading to trauma can leave a permanent scar on the mind, and as time passes by, users choose to reduce their pain by using drugs of their choice.

Such events include:

- Terrorism

- Accidents

- Natural disasters

- Physical abuse

- Sexual abuse

- Verbal abuse

- Neglect

2) Environment

It has been scientifically proven that genetics alone does not make one an addict. The home that your siblings and you were brought up in plays a big role in their addiction. Factors that play into this include:

- The regular argument at work or home

- Illness of the brain

- Divorce

- Alcohol abuse

- Drug addiction

3) Peer Pressure

People of the same social group are termed as peers.

Dialectical Behavioral Therapy (DBT)

This is a detailed cognitive behavioral treatment procedure. The therapy is mainly used to cure people that have little progress in other therapeutic treatment. It mainly focuses on solving issue-based and acceptance-based strategies. The treatment works in a holistic way of dialectical procedure. Dialectical refers to procedures that combine contrast concepts together such as acceptance and change.

It consists of five key components:

1. Generalization

The therapists use different formulas to motivate the transfer of skills learned throughout the program. They learn to use what was learned at school, at work, at home, and in the community. The learner can apply to regulate the emotion skills before and after the program.

2. Enhancing the capability

Gives chances for the improvement of learned existing skills. Basic skills sets are taught. These are:

- Interpersonal effectiveness
- Mindfulness
- Regulating Emotions
- Distress tolerance

3. Enhancing Motivation

Applies personalized behavior procedure to decrease difficult behaviors that cause negative effects on the quality of life.

4. **Environment Structuring**

The aim of the procedure is mostly to ensure positive and adaptive behaviors that are instilled throughout all environmental basics. E.g When a person is involved in multiple programs within one treating clinic, the doctor should ensure every step is set up to actualize all the right skills and behaviors taught.

5. **Motivational and Capability-enhancing of the Doctor**

Since DBT is often provided to people who experience severe, chronic, and intense mental health problems, therapists receive a big deal of supervision and support to prevent outcomes like burnout.

Dialectical Therapy in Alcohol and Drug Addiction

Help in Recovery from Substance Abuse

The main purpose of the therapy is to assist the addict to live a life worth living. This can be a very effective method of treating addiction if the addict has been battling with substance addiction and have not positively responded to other treatment by therapy.

Dialectical Therapy improves the seemingly contrasting goals of acceptance and change. Applying that way one step at a time and thus, learns to cope with day to day issues without going to the extreme emotional reaction that commonly leads to going back to substance abuse.

Focusing on Drug Addiction

Where the therapy is applied as a procedure of treating and changing substance abuse and addiction, a targeted goal on behavior which is similar to dependence on drugs, that is coming between an individual and his/her quality way of life.

Aims of therapy include:

- Reducing physical discomfort

- Reducing pain during the withdrawal stage

- Lowering cravings on the drug

- Refusing the idea to use drugs

- Learning to pursue personal goals and envisioning them all together

- Reducing the use of mind-altering substances such as alcohol that may lead you to use drugs again

- Recognizing things that make one go back to drugs and also avoiding those triggers

One other important thing is social support to the victims by the family members and the community at large.

Dialectical Therapy Works for Substance Addiction

These are the four main procedures that are combined to assist the addicts to get better from reliance on mind-altering drugs.

These procedures include:

- Use of phones whereby the addict is free to call and talk to the therapist when he/she feels vulnerable and needs advice.

- Consulting the doctor to feel more motivated.

- Training of skills is done in small groups.

- One-on-one sessions with a therapist which helps the addict to feel motivated and thus apply the new skills as taught.

Effectiveness of Therapy in Treating Alcohol Addiction and Drug Addiction

It is very effective in decreasing substance abuse as well as suicidal behavior and self-harming tendencies. Skills learned through the Therapy sessions help one learn to regulate their emotions, keep up with problematic situations, and also improve the relationships with the outside world. Those skills are very helpful in reducing the overreliance on substances and hence will help improve one starting to build a life worth living.

Exploring Early Phases of Addiction to Drugs and Alcohol

For most individuals, alcohol and drug abuse begin with experimental use in social contexts and younger age. Different drugs cause varying dependence levels. Alterations in sleeping habits and changed eating habits may signal high reliance on substance abuse. Individuals beginning to get hooked on drugs and alcohol may start caring less about their grooming as well as spending more time with persons who use drugs or drink excessively. Some of the signs of early addiction to drugs and alcohol include missing work, classes, or appointment commitments. A person beginning to get hooked on drugs and alcohol may start losing interest in activities that he or she used to enjoy. The other early symptoms of drugs and alcohol abuse include difficulties recognizing and abiding by laws and regulations that the individual previously had no challenges obeying.

Additional signs indicating drugs and alcohol addiction include experiencing an intense desire for the substance either once or severally during the day. Addiction to drugs and alcohol may make the individual want more of a substance to realize the same effect. A person hooked on drugs and alcohol tends to be fixated on ensuring that he or she secures a stable supply of the substance. Such persons will spend their income on drugs and alcohol even when the cost is beyond their reach. At times, individuals hooked on drugs and alcohol will spend less time engaging in social activities. Abuse of substance will lead to challenges on meeting family, work, or study responsibilities. People hooked on drugs and alcohol lie to friends and family about drug use or alcohol when asked to come clear of the suspicions leveled against them. Due to the strong impulse to secure and abuse drugs and alcohol, persons hooked on these substances may start engaging in illegal activities such as stealing to sustain the behavior.

Adverse Effects of Abusing Alcohol and Drugs

The continued use of drugs and alcohol affects almost every other part of your body. Drug abuse can induce heart attacks, collapse veins and contribute to infections of the heart valves. Abuse of drugs and alcohol affect your body physiologically, physically, and mentally. Physically, alcohol may slow down your coordination making you susceptible to falls and passing out. In this state, an individual that abuses alcohol is a danger to himself and the public especially if the person operates machinery or crosses the path of machinery. Some drugs can either excite an individual or incapacitate the individual making it hard to predict the movement and coordination of the person.

Correspondingly, substance abuse affects the mental status of a person making the decisions of such people erratic and unpredictable. Abuse of alcohol tends to compromise the decision-making process of a person, increasing the chances of the person making irrational decisions. Such decisions can include careless indulgence in risky sex or illegal activities such as crossing a busy road. The individual may be careful when sober but the person goes ahead to engage in random sex without using protection. Persons that abuse drugs may be willing to attempt anything to get their daily dosage including threatening their own children or pets. Abusing drugs may become more important than attending to children or watching over a cooking meal for a person hooked on cocaine.

Furthermore, individuals that abuse drugs suffer adverse physiological effects especially during the withdrawal period. The human body, when induced to substance abuse quickly, adjusts to operating with that level of the adjusted physiological state. Any slight drop in the biochemical levels will trigger crippling withdrawal symptoms making the person critically sick. The person abusing drugs and alcohol over time becomes a slave to these substances. In other terms, the individual has to be routinely recharged with drugs and alcohol to operate normally. Eliminating or reducing intake of drugs and alcohol will send a signal to the body that it is not in its threshold state and the body will trigger mechanisms to force the user to restore the adjusted biochemical levels, take drugs and alcohol.

Dialectical Behavior Therapy for Overcoming Substance Abuse

The qualification of using dialectical behavior therapy to overcome the abuse of alcohol and drugs is informed by what informs this behavior. Individuals abuse drugs and alcohol as a means of coping with anxiety, depression, and peer influence. The continued abuse of alcohol and drugs is possible since engaging in substance abuse can offer short-term solutions to depression, anxiety, and low self-esteem. Alcohol acts on the central nervous system as a depressant and lowers anxiety and stress, as well as produces feelings of relaxation and pleasure.

Unfortunately, the effects are temporary which implies that a person has to frequently engage in drinking to escape from anxiety and stress. Again, abusing alcohol also predisposes one to abuse drugs as a person may desire a more potent effect of calming anxiety and feel relaxed. Fortunately, dialectical behavior therapy can help address the push factors for abusing alcohol and drugs and offer a long-term solution to needing to engage in substance abuse.

Individuals grappling with substance abuse understand that they face shame and guilt and any intervention to assist their reform should include this element. Dialectical behavior therapy is most suited to address the issue of self-judgment and acceptability while offering cognitive behavioral therapy benefits. Acceptance that is invoked through applying dialectical behavior therapy can help boost the self-esteem of abusers of drugs and alcohol, a phenomenon that can help lower the need to engage in substance abuse to feel worthy and accepted. As we will demonstrate, dialectical behavior therapy advocates for creating a connection between the individual and dialectical behavior therapist. Through this bond, a healthy outlet for spiritual and emotional growth is offered.

Dialectical Behavior Therapy as a Remedy for Alcohol and Drug Addiction

Comprehending Dialectical Behavior Therapy

Notably, the efficacy of dialectical behavior therapy is that it is anchored on cognitive behavioral therapy concepts and is interpreted as a form of cognitive behavioral therapy. The main variation from cognitive behavior therapy is that dialectical behavior therapy integrates mindfulness of practices as well as a dialectical perspective to overcome alcohol and drug use. The concept of incorporating or balancing complete opposites to discover a middle ground is known as dialectical. In a way, dialectical behavior therapy extends the cognitive behavioral therapy model by allowing inclusion of dialectical and meditation aspects to the treatment plan. The dialectical behavior therapy approach argues for inviting the participation of the victim of an addiction to manage impulsive feelings, learn to accommodate stress, and develop desired interpersonal skills.

By understanding that alcohol and drug use is multifaceted, a multifaceted therapeutic approach should be invoked. Through dialectical behavior therapy, a victim of addiction is subjected to group sessions, individual therapy sessions, and weekly team consultations to get support. Addicts struggling with alcohol and drug use are battling two complete opposites where one extreme end wants to cease thinking and indulging in alcohol and drug use while the other desperately wants to participate in alcohol and drug abuse. Each of the extreme sides thinks that their needs are necessary and beneficial to the individual. Creating a middle ground would help the person feel less compelled to indulge in alcohol and drug abuse.

Furthermore, through dialectics, we start to view the problem from the victim's eyes rather than what we think. Dialectics allows us to grant the victim a chance to present the conflicting thoughts in their mind and why the alcohol and drug abuse thoughts end tends to win. By invoking dialectics we will allow the person suffering from alcohol and drug abuse to suggest ways of how we can gradually elevate the non-alcohol and drug abuse mind over the alcohol and drug abuse - oriented mind. The significant benefit of this phase in overcoming addiction is that we will allow the individual to demand treatment and participate in treatment. Most of the unsuccessful addiction rehabilitation programs are because the intended change does not emerge from the victim of addiction but rather the authority such as parents, spouses, or law enforcers. Dialectics avoid this fatal flaw by creating room for the continued participation of the participant at both mental and physical levels.

Arguably, dialectics sets the path for not judging the alcohol or drug abuse victim. Dialectics starts with the assumption that an individual is battling two extremes in his or her mind with the adverse extreme winning the dilemma. Through dialectics, we tend to accept that an addict of alcohol or drug abuse has space for wanting to stop engaging in the act but is unable to conquer the impulse to engage in alcohol or drug abuse. In a way, dialectics allows us to continue to view an addict as one of us, capable of what we can. Believing in a patient is critical to guiding the patient through the addiction. Most of the alcohol or drug abuse addicts are victims of the underlying circumstances that they have challenges overcoming which makes them prone to excessive alcohol or drug use.

Overcoming alcohol or drug abuse requires us to find new skills and apply them such as dialectical behavior therapy. The dialectical behavior therapy helps us to understand and qualify the reasons for the patient's indulgence in alcohol or drug abuse even though such individuals understand the addiction is destructive at personal and communal levels. Through dialectical behavior therapy, alcohol or drug abuse victims will feel validated and supported by recognizing the two opposing assumptions. The approach of dialectical behavior therapy is meant to help addicts of alcohol or drug use reconcile the internal conflict that emerges when we try to induce change as a treatment of addiction. The dialectical behavior therapy helps therapists find it easier to show compassion towards handling addicts of alcohol or drug use without getting frustrated.

Overcoming Substance Abuse using the Modules of Dialectical Behavior Therapy

Dialectical behavior therapy divides treatment into several modules with each module customized to elicit relief to the clients by allowing the addicts to build basic life skills that will make it easier to lead a happier and productive life. The modules are four in total and are intended to fill the inadequacies exhibited in individuals with alcohol or drug use addiction in this context. The dialectical behavior therapy modules are distress tolerance, core mindfulness, interpersonal effectiveness, and emotion regulation.

I.   Core Mindfulness Module

In this first module, a client is helped to build mindfulness skills such as helping a client become aware of self. One of the ways of becoming aware of self is to remain present at the moment and focus on your feelings, thoughts, and behaviors. It is important that the client learns to become mindful as this is required in subsequent modules of dialectical behavior therapy. The qualification for mindfulness skills is because alcohol or drug use addiction and indeed any other form of addiction are triggered by impulsivity as long as the underlying causes exist. The mindfulness module seeks to help an individual learn to restrain impulsive behavior which is a critical aspect of alcohol or drug abuse.

II.   Emotion Regulation Module

Lack of requisite emotional management is a prime factor in triggering alcohol or drug abuse. Individuals battling alcohol or drug abuse exhibit poor emotion regulation which pushes them to excessive alcohol or drug use as an escape from reality. Patients with addiction to alcohol or drug use in this module learn to detect, comprehend, and handle their emotions as well as lower their susceptibility to stressful emotions. Addicts of alcohol or drug use at this stage will learn how to recognize and assess emotional triggers such as how to interpret situations. It is important to walk through alcohol or drug use on ways of acting out their emotions and the impact of those behaviors.

III.   Distress Tolerance Module

Alcohol or drug abuse victims now need to become more receptive to their condition and less critical of themselves, and this is addressed in the distress tolerance module. Alcohol or drug abuse victims should learn on ways of tolerating stressful situations by letting themselves get distracted, soothe themselves, and walk through the situation devoid of self-judging. Individuals engaging in alcohol or drug abuse may have a low-stress threshold and build stress tolerance can help address the underlying cause of alcohol or drug abuse. Developing distress tolerance entails learning to manage and navigate crises without engaging in activities that aggravate the distress.

IV.   Interpersonal Effectiveness Module

The last module of dialectical behavior therapy, interpersonal effectiveness, seeks to impart effective interpersonal skills to an addict of alcohol or drug use. Persons battling alcohol or drug abuse may be highly sensitive to real or perceived rejection. The frustrations due to feeling abandoned may strain interpersonal relationships making the individual feel that the only thing available for him or her is alcohol or drug abuse. Fortunately, dialectical behavior therapy helps people indulging in alcohol or drug abuse develop appropriate boundaries, exhibit more assertiveness, and manage conflicts in a beneficial manner.

Means of Implementing Dialectical Behavior Therapy to Address Substance Abuse

I. Cognitive-Based Approach

It is important to address the specifics of implementing dialectical behavior therapy because erratic implementations will not help change the alcohol or drug abuse. As indicated earlier, dialectical behavior therapy is anchored in cognitive behavioral therapy. Therapists implementing dialectical behavior therapy have to work with their patients to identify adverse thought patterns, irrational beliefs, and erratic assumptions that compound the problems in the life of the individual leading to engaging in excessive alcohol or drug use. Persons faced with an alcohol or drug abuse may have a distorted view of life and its relevance. Therapists using dialectical behavior therapy should guide alcohol or drug use addicts to substitute problematic internal dialogue with self-talk where the self-talk is more objective and less judgmental. There are other cognitive behavioral therapy methods such as practicing new skills, exposure therapy, and contingency management as well as problem-solving can be incorporated in the implementation of dialectical behavior therapy.

II. Collaborative Approach

As a core aspect of dialectical behavior therapy, therapists helping alcohol or drug abuse victims have to work with the clients in a collaborative and nonjudgmental manner. Developing a working partnership with a client is a critical pillar of dialectical behavior therapy. The importance of this technique is to help create a relaxed environment for alcohol or drug use addicts to share their feelings in an open and honest manner. The addicts of alcohol or drug use are allowed to exhibit the interpersonal skills they have learned in conquering alcohol or drug use addiction by the safe and supportive environment created. Dialectical behavior therapists utilize this opportunity to educate and reinforce suitable boundaries to inform effective interpersonal skills and to signal adverse behaviors that negatively affect the therapeutic relationship. Notably, the therapeutic relationship can be exploited to educate the clients to hone skills advocated for in dialectical behavior therapy. For practice and reinforcing the skills learned, homework tasks should be given.

III. Support-driven Approach

Making both the client and the therapist feel supported is one of the primary goals of dialectical behavior therapy treatment. The qualification of support-oriented technique in dialectical behavior therapy is that individuals' self-esteem is enhanced when they feel assured of support and will relax their defenses. People are more teachable when they relax their defenses. Clients get to focus on their therapy goals in a supportive environment and this improves the treatment process. Periodic consultations with therapists can help provide invaluable information about the client and the alcohol or drug use addiction problem.

The Core Objectives when using Dialectical Behavior Therapy to Address Substance Abuse

For dialectical behavior therapy to work, it is important that a therapist and the client develop a shared view of these five objectives.

1. Enhance and empower the skills of the client such as distress tolerance and emotion regulation. The intent of this objective is to encourage frequent engagement in skills group sessions that can be weekly.

2. Ensure you generalize the client skills to her or his routine life that is the world beyond the therapeutic setting. The intent of this objective is to encourage training as part of individual therapy sessions. Alcohol or drug abuse clients should be taught new skills and guided practice of the skills as part of homework tasks in between counseling sessions.

3. Thirdly, there is a need to enhance the motivation of the client for change and depress the frequency and occurrence of adverse behaviors. The objective can be realized in individual therapy sessions with the client. Furthermore, therapists implementing dialectical behavior therapy can require clients to complete a weekly diary that acts as a form of self-management. Through the diary card, dialectical behavior therapists can follow the progress of the client in form of treatment goals such as reduction of types of alcohol or drug use. It is important to prioritize treatment goals for alcohol or drug abuse which may differ per affected individual but they should always begin with the most urgent such as reducing the time spent in secluding oneself for hours to indulge in alcohol or drug abuse to the least.

4. Empower and support the skills and motivation of the therapist. Most importantly, this dialectical behavior therapy objective can be attained by weekly therapist consultation meetings. Under this goal, we should aim to sustain and support the therapist, as the latter is the primary treatment provider for the client in the dialectical behavior therapy program. Just like any other person handling addiction patients, dialectical behavior therapists are susceptible to burnouts, doubts from clients, or deviation from objectivity and lose of objectivity. If any of these things happened, they would work against the progress of the client. For this reason, a dialectical behavior therapist should use weekly team meetings to share with other therapists with respect to treatment of the client including challenges encountered.

5. The last objective concerns aligning the treatment environment to aid the success of the client. Things that adversely affect the success of the patient completing treatment of alcohol or drug use addiction include issues with the setting of the therapy and flaws in the delivery of treatment. The intent of this objective is to ensure that dialectical behavior therapy aspects fit the selected treatment environment for the benefit of both the client and the therapists with more emphasis on the affected person.

Activating Dialectical Behavior Therapy Programs

The recommended way of implementing a dialectical behavior therapy area as follows:

1. Individual therapy sessions with a dialectical behavior therapist that are held weekly.

2. Making telephone contact with the main dialectical behavior therapist in between counseling sessions.

3. Having group therapy counseling sessions weekly that should last between two and two and a half hours. The group counseling sessions should concentrate on honing the skills discussed under the four modules. Another therapist other than the main therapist can lead the group sessions.

Summary

When tackling substance abuse, dialectical behavior therapy offers a pragmatic approach to understanding and overcoming addiction to alcohol or drug use. The skills imparted through dialectical behavior therapy can also help other areas of an individual's life. The dialectical behavior therapy is a highly formalized approach to treating addiction to substance abuse. Dialectical behavior therapy underscores the criticality of a nonjudgmental and supportive environment. For this reason, the dialectical behavior therapy approach encourages clients and therapists to form a collaborative counseling relationship. The provision for weekly consultation between therapists in a dialectical behavior therapy setting allows for peer to peer sharing that improves the quality of treatment offered and reduces burnout. Most importantly, dialectical behavior therapy should not be forced on everyone even though it is generic and can be invoked to any person grappling with alcohol or drug use addiction. It is also important that the dialectical behavior therapy gets implemented to every detail by qualified individuals to improve the likelihoods of successfully helping a substance abuser overcome the addiction.

Chapter 2: Overcoming Addictions to Porn via Dialectical Behavior Therapy

Understanding Why Porn is an Issue

In this chapter, we will first understand what porn addiction is, its effect, and how to use dialectical behavior therapy to combat porn addiction. As a subset of sex addiction, porn addiction occurs on a continuum of behaviors that are excessively engaged in and impact an individual's life. Even though addiction to porn is not a medically recognized term, it is an addiction as it is part of sexual addictions. Porn addiction is becoming a major concern due to the ease of access and convenience of engaging in porn. In recent years, porn is easily available in various forms such as erotic pictures, erotic audio, and videos that can be streamed or downloaded on portable devices such as laptops, tablets, and smartphones. Earphones additionally allow for the convenience of viewing porn including the existence of hundreds of databases with varied porn content. It is this ease of access and convenience of engaging in porn that aggravates porn addiction.

Equally important is that the debate on porn addiction becomes complicated as different people view the usage of porn differently unlike say cocaine. There is no quick consensus on the impact of porn on users. Some people argue that porn delivers healthy dosages while others think porn should be done away within society. Most individuals have watched or will watch in their lifetime. Sexual fantasies and sexual desires are integral to human life. Porn has become an issue mainly because technology is moderating the addiction especially on ease and convenience of access. At what point should one realize that he or she is now becoming hooked to porn and this informs the next paragraph of this discussion.

Qualifying one as an Addict of Porn

The attributes of porn addiction include excessive viewing of pornography material. In this context, excessive varies but essentially any increased viewing of porn that it starts interfering with an individual qualifies as excessive porn viewership. Porn addiction manifests when an individual's normal daily behavior gets disrupted adversely because of watching porn. For instance, when a student secludes himself to watch porn in his cubicle then the person is becoming a porn addict. A person will be categorized as getting addicted to porn when he or she spends more time viewing porn or looking for porn especially stimulating porn types to achieve arousal or to climax. You are addicted to pornography when you get emotional distress including feeling withdrawn when you stop watching porn.

Additionally, addiction to porn can manifest as continued indulgence in porn-watching regardless of adverse effects such as seclusion from society and changing sexual construction of women. Individuals exhibiting porn addiction may engage in compulsive masturbation. Porn addiction may also lead to sexual dysfunction such as premature ejaculation and impotence. Engaging in porn viewing until it adversely impacts your social life is a symptom of porn addiction. For instance, when an individual finds it difficult to become aroused by the partner including experiencing significant changes in sexual behavior between the victim and the partner then porn addiction is damaging. Another symptom of porn addiction occurs when the victim watches porn to alter his or her mood as well as escaping from reality.

Causes of Addiction to Porn

Addiction to porn can be comprehended by invoking operant conditioning in psychology. The phenomenon operant conditioning arises when a specific behavior such as viewing porn gets reinforced, motivating you to desire to engage in it repeatedly. While different things can be rewarding leading to impact on our behavior, porn dominates reinforcement due to the reward that it offers that excites instinctual sex drive. For this reason, it is easier to get hooked on porn as it is tapping into a fundamental and fulfilling natural drive. Then another reason for high addictiveness of porn is that it is easier to access and enjoy it compared to other activities that lead to addiction such as drug use. Individuals who engage in porn find it a lesser evil and less demanding than going out to look for a partner. Porn addiction arises when seeking sexual pleasure becomes impulsive, excessive or occurs at the expense of other beneficial behaviors.

Further causes of porn addiction include an individual having a genetic propensity to impulsive behavior or sensation-seeking behavior. An individual with a propensity to other attributes linked to sexual addiction such as depression or anxiety is also likely to easily get addicted to porn. Higher levels of sex hormones such as testosterone or estrogen can impact libido thus lead to sex addiction behaviors such as watching porn excessively. Formative years exposed to environmental factors such as exposure to explicit content or abuse can help trigger underlying attributes in porn addiction behaviors. Poor mental health can contribute to desire to escape from reality and porn watching may offer the easy and convenient path out of anxiety, personality disorders, depression, performance anxiety, poor impulse control, and a horde of other mental health issues.

Correspondingly, the social causes of porn addiction are varied and include rejection in relationships as well as social circles. The rejection experienced in social circles and relationships can push an individual to watch porn excessively to achieve sexual gratification. When an individual is isolated socially, the person will have a higher likelihood of wanting unconventional ways to realize sexual gratification. Social isolation can also cause depression which has been argued that it contributes to porn addiction as the victim looks for a quick escape from reality. Peer influence as a social contributor to porn addiction occurs when a person engages in watching porn because friends are watching and the person wants to fit in the group.

Impact of Porn Addiction

Addiction to porn, as seen by what causes porn addiction, leads to adverse effects on a personal level and those around the individual. Physically, porn addiction can cause sexual dysfunction such as premature ejaculation and impotence. Psychologically, addiction to porn can lead to a preoccupation with sexual thoughts the entire day. When one person gets addicted to porn, that person will feel confused, ashamed, and guilty. Porn addiction can induce or worsen anxiety and depression especially if a person fears being caught such as engaging in porn watching in office, at school, and at home. Socially, addiction to porn can cause the victim to feel as if they do not need a real person for sexual engagement including depressed patients for sexual contact such as wanting to have sex outright. A person addicted to porn may experience a decline in sexual interactions with the partner such as emotional detachment. Fortunately, porn addiction can be detected and treated and this is what informs the next segment of this chapter.

Dialectical Behavior Therapy as a Remedy for Porn Addiction

Understanding Dialectical Behavior Therapy

The power of dialectical behavior therapy is that it is anchored on cognitive behavioral therapy concepts and is interpreted as a form of cognitive behavioral therapy. The major variation from cognitive behavior therapy is that dialectical behavior therapy integrates mindfulness practices as well as a dialectical viewpoint to combating porn addiction. The concept of incorporating or balancing complete opposites to discover a middle ground is known as dialectical. In this regard, dialectical behavior therapy extends the cognitive behavioral therapy model by allowing inclusion of dialectical and meditation aspects to the treatment plan. The dialectical behavior therapy approach argues for inviting the participation of the victim of an addiction to manage impulsive feelings, learn to accommodate stress and develop desired interpersonal skills.

Since porn addiction is multifaceted, a multifaceted therapeutic approach is only expected. Through dialectical behavior therapy, a victim of addiction is subjected to group sessions, individual therapy sessions, and weekly team consultations to get support. Persons struggling with porn addiction are battling two complete opposites where one end wants to cease thinking and watching porn while the other desperately wants to participate in watching porn. Each of the opposite sides thinks that their needs are necessary and beneficial to the individual. Finding a middle ground would help the person feel less compelled to viewing porn.

Through dialectics, we begin to understand the problem from the victim's eyes rather than what we think. Dialectics allows us to let the victim present conflicting thoughts in their mind and why the porn thoughts end tends to win. Using dialectics, we will allow the person suffering from porn addiction to suggest ways of how we can gradually elevate the non-porn mind over the porn-oriented mind. The significant benefit of this step-in battling addiction is that we will allow the individual to demand treatment and participate in treatment. Most of the unsuccessful addiction rehabilitation programs are because the intended change does not emerge from the victim of addiction but rather the authority such as parents, spouses, or law enforcers. Dialectics avoid this fatal flaw by creating room for the continued participation of the participant at both mental and physical levels.

Additionally, dialectics sets a path for not judging a porn addict. Dialectics starts with the assumption that an individual is battling two extremes in his or her mind with the adverse extreme winning the dilemma. Through dialectics, we tend to accept that an addict of porn has space for wanting to stop engaging in the act but is unable to conquer the impulse to watch porn. In other terms, dialectics allows us to continue believing that an addict is one of us, capable of what we can. Believing in a patient is critical to guiding the patient through the addiction. Most porn addicts are victims of the underlying circumstances that they have challenges conquering which makes them vulnerable to excessive watching of porn.

Combating porn addiction requires us to discover new skills and apply them such as dialectical behavior therapy. The dialectical behavior therapy helps us to comprehend and qualify the reasons for the patient's indulgence in porn addiction even though such individuals understand the addiction is destructive at personal and communal levels. Through dialectical behavior therapy, an addict of porn will feel validated and supported by recognizing the two opposing assumptions. The approach of dialectical behavior therapy is meant to help addicts of porn reconcile the internal conflict that emerges when we try to induce change as a treatment of addiction. The dialectical behavior therapy helps therapists find it easier to show compassion towards handling addicts of porn without getting frustrated.

Handling Porn Addict using the Modules of Dialectical Behavior Therapy

Dialectical behavior therapy divides treatment into several modules with each module customized to elicit relief to the clients by allowing the addicts to build basic life skills that will make it easier to lead a happier and productive life. The modules are four in total and are intended to fill the inadequacies exhibited in individuals with porn addiction in this context. The dialectical behavior therapy modules are distress tolerance, core mindfulness, interpersonal effectiveness, and emotion regulation.

I.   Core Mindfulness Module

In this first module, a client is helped to build mindfulness skills such as helping a client become aware of self. One of the ways of becoming aware of self is to remain present at the moment and focus on your feelings, thoughts, and behaviors. It is important that the client learns to become mindful as this is required in subsequent modules of dialectical behavior therapy. The qualification for mindfulness skills is because porn addiction and indeed any other form of addiction are triggered by impulsivity as long as the underlying causes exist. The mindfulness module seeks to help an individual learn to restrain impulsive behavior which is a critical aspect of porn addiction.

II.   Emotion Regulation Module

Lack of requisite emotional management is a prime factor in triggering addiction to porn. Individuals battling an addiction to porn exhibit poor emotion regulation which pushes them to excessive watching of porn as an escape from reality. Patients with addiction to porn in this module learn to detect, comprehend, and handle their emotions as well as lower their susceptibility to stressful emotions. Addicts of porn at this stage will learn how to recognize and assess emotional triggers such as how to interpret situations. It is important to walk through porn addicts on ways of acting out their emotions and the impact of those behaviors.

III.   Distress Tolerance Module

Addicts of porn now need to become more receptive to their condition and less critical of themselves and this is what the distress tolerance module addresses. Porn addicts should learn on ways of tolerating stressful situations by letting themselves get distracted, soothe themselves, and walk through the situation devoid of self-judging. Individuals with porn addiction may have a low-stress threshold and build stress tolerance can help address the underlying cause of porn addiction. Developing distress tolerance entails learning to manage and navigate crises without engaging in activities that aggravate the distress.

IV.   Interpersonal Effectiveness Module

The last module of dialectical behavior therapy, interpersonal effectiveness, seeks to impart effective interpersonal skills to an addict of porn. Persons battling porn addiction may be highly sensitive to real or perceived rejection. The frustrations due to feeling abandoned may strain interpersonal relationships making the individual feel the only thing available is porn. Fortunately, dialectical behavior therapy helps porn addicts develop appropriate boundaries, exhibit more assertiveness, and manage conflicts in a beneficial manner.

Ways of Implementing Dialectical Behavior Therapy to Address Porn Addiction

I. Cognitive-Based Approach

It is important to address the specifics of implementing dialectical behavior therapy because erratic implementations will not help change the addiction to porn. As indicated earlier, dialectical behavior therapy is anchored in cognitive behavioral therapy. Therapists implementing dialectical behavior therapy have to work with their patients to identify adverse thought patterns, irrational beliefs, and erratic assumptions that compound the problems in the life of the individual leading to engaging in excessive watching of porn. Persons faced with porn addiction may have a distorted view of sex and its relevance. Therapists using dialectical behavior therapy should guide porn addicts to substitute problematic internal dialogue with self-talk that is more objective and less judgmental. Other cognitive behavioral therapy methods such as practicing new skills, exposure therapy, and contingency management, as well as problem-solving, can be incorporated in the implementation of dialectical behavior therapy.

II. Collaborative Approach

As a core aspect of dialectical behavior therapy, therapists helping porn addicts have to work with the clients in a collaborative and nonjudgmental manner. Forming a working partnership with a client is a critical pillar of dialectical behavior therapy. The importance of this technique is to help create a relaxed environment for porn addicts to share their feelings in an open and honest manner. The addicts of porn are allowed to exhibit the interpersonal skills they have learned in conquering porn addiction by the safe and supportive environment created. Dialectical behavior therapists utilize this opportunity to educate and reinforce suitable boundaries to inform effective interpersonal skills and to signal adverse behaviors that negatively affect the therapeutic relationship. Indeed, the therapeutic relationship can be exploited to educate the clients to hone skills advocated for in dialectical behavior therapy. For practice and reinforcing the skills learned, homework tasks should be given.

III.   Support-driven Approach

Making both the client and the therapist feel supported is one of the main goals of dialectical behavior therapy treatment. The qualification of support-oriented technique in dialectical behavior therapy is that individuals' self-esteem is enhanced when they feel assured of support and will relax their defenses. People are more teachable when they drop their defenses. Clients get to concentrate on their therapy targets in a supportive environment and this improves the treatment process. Periodic consultations with therapists can help provide invaluable information about the client and the porn addiction problem.

Developing Objectives using Dialectical Behavior Therapy to Overcome Porn Addiction

For dialectical behavior therapy to work, it is important that a therapist and the client develop a shared view of these five objectives.

1. Enhance and empower the skills of the client such as distress tolerance and emotion regulation. The intent of this objective is to encourage frequent engagement in skills group sessions that can be weekly.

2. Ensure you generalize the client skills to her or his routine life that is the world beyond the therapeutic setting. The intent of this objective is to encourage training as part of individual therapy sessions. Porn addicts should be taught new skills and guided practice of the skills as part of homework tasks in between counseling sessions.

3. Thirdly, there is a need to enhance the motivation of the client for change and depress the frequency and occurrence of adverse behaviors. The objective can be realized in individual therapy sessions with the client. Furthermore, therapists implementing dialectical behavior therapy can require clients to complete a weekly diary that acts as a form of self-management. Through the diary card, dialectical behavior therapists can follow the progress of the client in form of treatment goals such as reduction of types of porn videos watched. It is important to prioritize treatment goals for porn addiction which may differ per client but they should always begin with the most urgent such as reducing the time spent in secluding oneself for hours to watch porn to the least.

4. Empower and support the skills and motivation of the therapist. Most importantly, this dialectical behavior therapy objective can be attained by weekly therapist consultation meetings. Under this goal, we should aim to sustain and support the therapist as the latter is the primary treatment provider for the client in the dialectical behavior therapy program. Just like any other person handling addiction patients, dialectical behavior therapists are susceptible to burnouts, doubts from clients, or deviation from objectivity and lose of objectivity. If any of these things happened, they would work against the progress of the client. For this reason, a dialectical behavior therapist should use weekly team meetings to share with other therapists with respect to

treatment of the client including challenges encountered.

5. The last objective concerns aligning the treatment environment to aid the success of the client. Things that adversely affect the success of the patient completing treatment of porn addiction include issues with the setting of the therapy and flaws in the delivery of treatment. The intent of this objective is to ensure that dialectical behavior therapy aspects fit the selected treatment environment for the benefit of both the client and the therapists with more emphasis on the client.

Implementing Dialectical Behavior Therapy Programs

The standard way of implementing dialectical behavior therapy is as follows:

1. Individual therapy sessions with a dialectical behavior therapist that are held weekly.
2. Making telephone contact with the main dialectical behavior therapist in between counseling sessions.
3. Having group therapy counseling sessions weekly that should last between two and two and a half hours. The group counseling sessions should concentrate on honing the skills discussed under the four modules. Another therapist other than the main therapist can lead the group sessions.

Qualification of Dialectical Behavior Therapy

Dialectical behavior therapy offers a pragmatic approach to understanding and overcoming addiction to porn. The skills gained through dialectical behavior therapy can also help other areas of an individual's life. The dialectical behavior therapy is highly formalized approach to treating porn addiction. Dialectical behavior therapy underscores the criticality of a nonjudgmental and supportive environment. For this reason, the dialectical behavior therapy approach encourages clients and therapists to form a collaborative counseling relationship. The provision for weekly consultation between therapists in a dialectical behavior therapy setting allows for peer to peer sharing that improves the quality of treatment offered and reduces burnout. Most importantly, dialectical behavior therapy should not be forced on everyone even though it is generic and can be invoked to any person grappling with porn addiction. It is also important that dialectical behavior therapy gets implemented to every detail by qualified individuals to improve the likelihoods of successfully helping a porn addict overcome porn addiction.

Summary

In this chapter, we covered what constitutes porn addiction, its effect, and how to use dialectical behavior therapy to combat porn addiction. As a subset of sex addiction, porn addiction occurs on a continuum of behaviors that are excessively engaged in and impact an individual's life. Even though addiction to porn is not a medically recognized term, it is an addiction as it is part of sexual addictions. Porn addiction has become a major concern due to the ease of access and convenience of engaging in porn. In recent years porn is easily available in various forms such as erotic pictures, erotic audio, and videos that can be streamed or downloaded on portable devices such as laptops, tablets, and smartphones.

Therefore, the power of dialectical behavior therapy is that it is anchored on cognitive behavioral therapy concepts and is interpreted as a form of cognitive behavioral therapy. The major variation from cognitive behavior therapy is that dialectical behavior therapy integrates mindfulness practices as well as a dialectical viewpoint to combating porn addiction. The concept of incorporating or balancing complete opposites to discover a middle ground is known as dialectical. In this regard, dialectical behavior therapy extends the cognitive behavioral therapy model by allowing inclusion of dialectical and meditation aspects to the treatment plan. The dialectical behavior therapy approach argues for inviting the participation of the victim of an addiction to manage impulsive feelings, learn to accommodate stress and develop desired interpersonal skills.

Chapter 3: Employing Dialectical Behavior Therapy to Overcome Online Gambling Addiction

Understanding what Online Gambling Addiction is

Addiction to gambling can be classified as a psychiatric disorder when an individual exhibit any of the recognized symptoms. A person is deemed as addicted to gambling when he or she is preoccupied with gambling. The person may relive past gambling exercises, plan for the next session of gambling, or devise means of getting the fund to gamble. The other signal that one is an addict of online gambling arises when the person has an impulse to spend a significant amount of money to attain the desired level of excitement. Engaging in multiple abortive attempts to stop or lower gambling is a symptom of addiction to online gambling. Individuals addicted to online gambling tend to become restless and irritable when attempting to stop or lessen gambling habits. When online gambling is perceived as a means of escaping from reality, then it is a sign of addiction to gambling. A person is addicted to online gambling when he or she starts chasing losses.

Additionally, individuals addicted to online gambling will lie to employers, family, and friends as an attempt to mask the time or funds lost while gambling. With time, a person addicted to online gambling will experience difficulties in endeavors that require commitment such as academic and relationship. Depending on others for funds to gamble is another attribute of addiction to online gambling. As indicated, persons suffering from compulsive gambling are at risk of financial, work, legal, and financial problems. Addiction to online gambling has been associated with panic disorder, anxiety, depression, and personality disorders. Excessive indulgence in gambling can lead to a drug, nicotine, and online gambling dependence, and in some cases suicide. Family members are also affected by a member who indulges in gambling

Why Online Gambling Worsens Addiction

Online gambling gets more focus as they are different aspects of gambling that makes it highly addictive compared to gambling from a physical location. In this aspect, technology is a moderating factor to gambling which increases the risk of addiction. First, online gambling worsens addiction because of the convenience of access. A gambler can easily access the gambling site anywhere and at any time as long there is internet coverage. On the other hand, it would take significant effort to access a physical location venue and not all are operational throughout the day.

Secondly, the physical casino has a capacity of people they can allow to gamble at a time, unlike online gambling where capacity is insatiable. Thirdly, online gambling offers a perfect hideout when engaging in gambling, unlike physical location gambling where those around a person can notice the unusual behavior and induce help to the addict.

Furthermore, physical location gambling offers plenty of distractions to the gambler as the place is filled with other people and different services. On the other hand, online gambling is devoid of much of the distractions present in a physical location making a gambler concentrate more on gambling. Additionally, online gambling allows placing bets of far smaller amounts of money that physical casinos would not accept. The result of allowing smaller units of gambling is that it mops up the threshold of operating, throwing the gambler deeper into the adverse effects of gambling. As earlier indicated, online gambling denies the gambler alternative voices of reason as the individual is engaging in gambling anonymously and probably alone at home.

Another attribute of online gambling that worsens addiction includes the ease of accessing funds in bank account online whereas physical location gambling creates inconvenience of having to withdraw the money from the bank. For this reason, online gambling increases the chances of impulse gambling as well as chasing losses. Chasing losses in gambling occurs when a gambler immediately gambles again with the aim of recovering lost money but ends up losing more and again stakes more to recover the combined losses. Then the online monetary transaction may fool one to think that the money being spent is not real money. Sometimes gamblers may use overdraft provisions to stake in their daily gamblers not realizing how deep they are digging a financial hole.

Correspondingly while online gambling sites may be legal, and are operating legally, the industry might be poorly regulated. It is also difficult to determine who is behind a certain online gambling firm making it hard to hold such individuals to law and ethical expectations. For instance, it is relatively easy for physical casinos to restrict entry and participation of minors or problems of losing control, unlike online gambling sites. Even though online gambling sites have well-formulated policies and regulations, it is not clear how they implement the regulations. In most cases, internet gambling sites leave the burden of limiting gambling to the individual user leading to an obsession with gambling to overcome willpower to manage to gamble.

For this reason, remedying online gambling addiction will require recognizing the underlying factors that inform the excessive indulgence. As illustrated, online gambling increases chances of anonymity, seclusion, convenience and access to gambling site and funds. On its account, online money increases the likelihood of unplanned spending as well as increased the frequency of spending funds. When online gambling connects to electronic money then adverse effects are compounded. In other terms, the physical, social and mental factors that exist favor continued indulgence in online gambling. It then emerges that to understand and overcome online gambling there is a need for an approach that is comprehensive, aggressive, and multifaceted such as dialectic behavioral therapy.

Dialectical Behavior Therapy to Overcome Online Gambling

The Concept of Dialectical Behavior Therapy

Online gambling requires an aggressive, comprehensive, and responsive approach and this is what dialectic behavior therapy offers. The dialectic behavioral therapy relies on the efficacy of the model that it is anchored on cognitive behavioral therapy concepts and is interpreted as a form of cognitive behavioral therapy. The main variation from cognitive behavior therapy is that dialectical behavior therapy integrates mindfulness practices as well as a dialectical perspective to overcome an online gambling addiction. The concept of incorporating or balancing complete opposites to discover a middle ground is known as dialectical. In a way, dialectical behavior therapy extends the cognitive behavioral therapy model by allowing inclusion of dialectical and meditation aspects to the treatment plan. The dialectical behavior therapy approach argues for inviting the participation of the victim of an addiction to manage impulsive feelings, learn to accommodate stress and develop desired interpersonal skills.

Among other approaches, battling online gambling addiction will require increasing social interaction of the addict. Most of the individuals that engage in online gambling are trying to escape from anxiety, pressure, expectations, and disappointment in life. Online gambling seems to provide much-needed space and preoccupation for online gambling addicts. It is important to disrupt the perfect environment for online gambling by finding ways to help the individual defuse depression, anxiety, and disappointments. The therapy should empower the individual to learn ways of ignoring the temptation to engage in online gambling by letting the person discover other things that can be done when alone and online.

By understanding that online gambling addiction is multifaceted, a multifaceted therapeutic approach should be invoked. Through dialectical behavior therapy, a victim of addiction is subjected to group sessions, individual therapy sessions, and weekly team consultations to get support. Addicts struggling with online gambling addictions are battling two complete opposites where one extreme end wants to cease thinking and indulging in online gambling addiction while the other desperately wants to participate in online gambling addiction. Each of the extreme sides thinks that their needs are necessary and beneficial to the individual. Creating a middle ground would help the person feel less compelled to indulge in online gambling addiction.

Through group activities and collaboration, addicts of online gambling can share and relate to each other and with the therapists. Like any other form of addiction, online gamblers that are battling addiction share a lot with other online gamblers having the same problem. For instance, most of these individuals think online gambling may offer a quick way out of their financial misery. Groups of people facing online gambling addiction may wrongly believe that they will recover from the huge losses and quit the destructive habit. Most of the online gambling addicts wish to stop the habit but need to leave with some dignity such as recovering the losses made. The groups offer an opportunity to share challenges and encourage each other.

For emphasis, it is important to walk through the problem of online gambling addiction through the eyes of the addict. Fortunately, through dialectics, we start to view the problem from the victim's eyes rather than what we think. Dialectics allows us to grant the victim a chance to present the conflicting thoughts in their mind and why the online gambling addiction thoughts end tends to win. By invoking dialectics, we will allow the person suffering from online gambling addiction to suggest ways of how we can gradually elevate the nation- online gambling addiction mind over the online gambling addiction -oriented mind. The significant benefit of this phase in overcoming addiction is that we will allow the individual to demand treatment and participate in treatment. Most of the unsuccessful addiction rehabilitation programs are because the intended change does not emerge from the victim of addiction but rather the authority such as parents, spouses, or law enforcers. Dialectics avoid this fatal flaw by creating room for the continued participation of the participant at both mental and physical levels.

Notably, it is important to create an environment that encourages openness and connection for the addicts of online gambling to freely share their fears and aspirations. Dialectics sets the path for not judging an online gambling addiction victim. Dialectics starts with the assumption that an individual is battling two extremes in his or her mind with the adverse extreme winning the dilemma. Through dialectics, we tend to accept that an addict of online gambling addiction online gambling addiction has space for wanting to stop engaging in the act but is unable to conquer the impulse to engage in online gambling addiction. In a way, dialectics allows us to continue an addict as one of us capable of what we can. Believing in a patient is critical to guiding the patient through the addiction. Most of the online gambling addiction addicts are victims of the underlying circumstances that they have challenges overcoming which makes them prone to excessive online gambling addiction.

Conquering online gambling addiction requires us to find new skills and apply them such as dialectical behavior therapy. The dialectical behavior therapy helps us to understand and qualify the reasons for the patient's indulgence in online gambling addiction even though such individuals understand the addiction is destructive at personal and communal levels. Through dialectical behavior therapy, online gambling addiction victims will feel validated and supported by recognizing the two opposing assumptions. The approach of dialectical behavior therapy is meant to help addicts of online gambling addiction reconcile the internal conflict that emerges when we try to induce change as a treatment of addiction. The dialectical behavior therapy helps therapists find it easier to show compassion towards handling addicts of online gambling addiction without getting frustrated.

Overcoming Substance Abuse using the Modules of Dialectical Behavior Therapy
Dialectical behavior therapy divides treatment into several modules with each module customized to elicit relief to the clients by allowing the addicts to build basic life skills that will make it easier to lead a happier and productive life. The modules are four in total and are intended to fill the inadequacies exhibited in individuals with online gambling addiction in this context. The dialectical behavior therapy modules are distress tolerance, core mindfulness, interpersonal effectiveness, and emotion regulation.

I.   Core Mindfulness Module

In this first module, a client is helped to build mindfulness skills such as helping a client become aware of self. One of the ways of becoming aware of self is to remain present at the moment and focus on your feelings, thoughts, and behaviors. It is important that the client learns to become mindful as this is required in subsequent modules of dialectical behavior therapy. The qualification for mindfulness skills is because online gambling addiction and indeed any other form of addiction is triggered by impulsivity as long as the underlying causes exist. The mindfulness module seeks to help an individual learn to restrain impulsive behavior which is a critical aspect of online gambling addiction.

II.   Emotion Regulation Module

Lack of requisite emotional management is a prime factor in triggering online gambling addiction. Individuals battling online gambling addiction exhibit poor emotion regulation which pushes them to excessive online gambling addiction as an escape from reality. Patients with addiction to online gambling, in this module, will learn to detect, comprehend, and handle their emotions as well as lower their susceptibility to stressful emotions. Addicts of online gambling addiction at this stage will learn how to recognize and assess emotional triggers such as how to interpret situations. It is important to walk through online gambling addiction on ways of acting out their emotions and the impact of those behaviors.

III. Distress Tolerance Module

Online gambling addiction victims now need to become more receptive to their condition and less critical of themselves and this is what the distress tolerance module addresses. Online gambling addiction victims should learn on ways of tolerating stressful situations by letting themselves get distracted, soothe themselves, and walk through the situation devoid of self-judging. Individuals engaging in online gambling addiction may have a low-stress threshold and building stress tolerance can help address the underlying cause of online gambling addiction. Developing distress tolerance entails learning to manage and navigate crises without engaging in activities that aggravate the distress.

IV. Interpersonal Effectiveness Module

The last module of dialectical behavior therapy, interpersonal effectiveness, seeks to impart effective interpersonal skills to an addict of online gambling. Persons battling online gambling addiction may be highly sensitive to real or perceived rejection. The frustrations due to feeling abandoned may strain interpersonal relationships making the individual feel the only thing available for him or her is online gambling addiction. Fortunately, dialectical behavior therapy helps people indulging in online gambling addiction develop appropriate boundaries, exhibit more assertiveness, and manage conflicts in a beneficial manner.

Means of Implementing Dialectical Behavior Therapy to Address Substance Abuse

I.   Cognitive-Based Approach

It is important to address the specifics of implementing dialectical behavior therapy because erratic implementations will not help change the online gambling addiction. As indicated earlier, dialectical behavior therapy is anchored in cognitive behavioral therapy. Therapists implementing dialectical behavior therapy have to work with their patients to identify adverse thought patterns, irrational beliefs, and erratic assumptions that compound the problems in the life of the individual leading to engaging in excessive online gambling addiction. Persons faced with an online gambling addiction may have a distorted view of life and its relevance. Therapists using dialectical behavior therapy should guide online gambling addiction addicts to substitute problematic internal dialogue with self-talk and make the individual feel less judgmental. There are other cognitive behavioral therapy methods such as practicing new skills, exposure therapy, and contingency management as well as problem-solving can be incorporated in the implementation of dialectical behavior therapy.

II.   Collaborative Approach

As a core aspect of dialectical behavior therapy, therapists helping online gambling addiction victims have to work with the clients in a collaborative and nonjudgmental manner. Developing a working partnership with a client is a critical pillar of dialectical behavior therapy. The importance of this technique is to help create a relaxed environment for online gambling addicts to share their feelings in an open and honest manner. These addicts are allowed to exhibit the interpersonal skills they have learned in conquering online gambling addiction by the safe and supportive environment created. Dialectical behavior therapists utilize this opportunity to educate and reinforce suitable boundaries to inform effective interpersonal skills and to signal adverse behaviors that negatively affect the therapeutic relationship. Notably, the therapeutic relationship can be exploited to educate the clients to hone skills advocated for in dialectical behavior therapy. For practice and reinforcing the skills learned, homework tasks should be given.

III.   Support-driven Approach

Making both the client and the therapist feel supported is one of the primary goals of dialectical behavior therapy treatment. The qualification of support-oriented technique in dialectical behavior therapy is that individuals' self-esteem is enhanced when they feel assured of support and will relax their defenses. People are more teachable when they relax their defenses. Clients get to focus on their therapy goals in a supportive environment and this improves the treatment process. Periodic consultations with therapists can help provide invaluable information about the client and the online gambling addiction problem.

The Core Objectives when using Dialectical Behavior Therapy to Address Substance Abuse

For dialectical behavior therapy to work, it is important that a therapist and the client develop a shared view of these five objectives.

1. Enhance and empower the skills of the client such as distress tolerance and emotion regulation. The intent of this objective is to encourage frequent engagement in skills group sessions that can be weekly.
2. Ensure you generalize the client skills to her or his routine life that is the world beyond the therapeutic setting. The intent of this objective is to encourage training as part of individual therapy sessions. Online gambling addiction clients should be taught new skills and guided practice of the skills as part of homework tasks in between counseling sessions.
3. Thirdly, there is a need to enhance the motivation of the client for change and depress the frequency and occurrence of adverse behaviors. The objective can be realized in individual therapy sessions with the client. Furthermore, therapists implementing dialectical behavior therapy can require clients to complete a weekly diary that acts as a form of self-management. Through the diary card, dialectical behavior therapists can follow the progress of the client in form of treatment goals such as reduction of types of online gambling addiction. It is important to prioritize treatment goals for online gambling addiction which may differ per affected individual but they should always begin with the most urgent such as reducing the time spent in secluding oneself for hours to indulge in online gambling addiction to the least.
4. Empower and support the skills and motivation of the therapist. Most importantly, this dialectical behavior therapy objective can be attained by weekly therapist consultation meetings. Under this goal, we should aim to sustain and support the therapist as the latter is the primary treatment provider for the client in the dialectical behavior therapy program. Just like any other person handling addiction patients, dialectical behavior therapists are susceptible to burnouts, doubts

from clients, or deviation from objectivity and lose of objectivity. If any of these things happened, they would work against the progress of the client. For this reason, a dialectical behavior therapist should use weekly team meetings to share with other therapists with respect to treatment of the client including challenges encountered.

5. The last objective concerns aligning the treatment environment to aid the success of the client. Things that adversely affect the success of the patient completing treatment of online gambling addiction include issues with the setting of the therapy and flaws in the delivery of treatment. The intent of this objective is to ensure that dialectical behavior therapy aspects fit the selected treatment environment for the benefit of both the client and the therapists with more emphasis on the affected person.

Activating Dialectical Behavior Therapy Programs

The recommended way of implementing a dialectical behavior therapy area as follows:

1. Individual therapy sessions with a dialectical behavior therapist that are held weekly.
2. Making telephone contact with the main dialectical behavior therapist in between counseling sessions.
3. Having group therapy counseling sessions weekly that should last between two and two and a half hours. The group counseling sessions should concentrate on honing the skills discussed under the four modules. Another therapist other than the main therapist can lead the group sessions.

Summary

When tackling substance abuse, dialectical behavior therapy offers a pragmatic approach to understanding and overcoming addiction to online gambling. The skills imparted through dialectical behavior therapy can also help other areas of an individual's life. The dialectical behavior therapy is a highly formalized approach to treating addiction to substance abuse. Dialectical behavior therapy underscores the criticality of a nonjudgmental and supportive environment. For this reason, the dialectical behavior therapy approach encourages clients and therapists to form a collaborative counseling relationship. The provision for weekly consultation between therapists in a dialectical behavior therapy setting allows for peer to peer sharing that improves the quality of treatment offered and reduces burnout. Most importantly, dialectical behavior therapy should not be forced on everyone even though it is generic and can be invoked to any person grappling with online gambling addiction. It is also important the dialectical behavior therapy gets implemented to every detail by qualified individuals to improve the likelihoods of successfully helping a substance abuser overcome the addiction.

Chapter 4: Employing Dialectical Behavior Therapy to Overcome Food Addiction

Food addiction happens when a person's appetite to eat becomes compulsive and cannot be controlled easily. Its compulsiveness state is in response to emotional needs such as anger, sadness, or stress.

Man need food to survive and be able to have the energy for the full functionality of the body but the addiction part is when an individual is overdependent on a certain type of food which is normally unhealthy, or not fit for the body in large amounts.

The Aspect of Food Addiction

It may really be an addiction to the behavior of eating. This is nearly related to consumption disorders such as binge eating disorder, and obesity.
A theory claims that people may develop chemical reliance on a specific food in a similar manner where individuals develop an addiction to cigarettes and alcohol.

A chemical known as dopamine in the brain is triggered when consuming food. The dopamine acts as a reward that gives a pleasurable feeling to the person consuming the food. When this chemical component is released in too many quantities, it becomes unhealthy to the brain.

Foods Closely Associated to Food Addiction

Studies show that foods that are rich in starch, sugar, and fat are more susceptible to or associated with food addiction. Some of the foods that are most problematic include:

- Chocolate
- Ice cream
- White bread
- Fries
- Chips
- Pasta
- Candy

Signs of being a Food Addict

Too much craving and being obsessive or preoccupied with consuming a particular type of food is a sign of being a food addict.
These symptoms may be social, emotional, and physical:

1. Consuming food to a level that there is physical pain.
2. Consuming food in secrecy or alone to avoid attention.
3. Having the urge to eat food for the purpose of emotional release.
4. Having no control over the number of times you need to eat.
5. Having no control over the amount of food being consumed and where it is being consumed.
6. Compulsive eating.
7. Several failed attempts to quit too much eating or overeating.
8. Just thinking about how to get more food, and eating.

Addiction to food can also cause physical consequences such as self-induced vomiting, compulsive exercise, and also too much of food restriction.

Ways of overcoming food addiction

- Accepting that he/she has a problem
- Agreeing to have a counseling or therapy session where you will say it all openly on why you need to control food
- By submitting yourself to nutrition counseling where the doctor will help you in understanding the negative impacts of bad food habits.
- Being open to people who love and care about you and letting them know everything being honest to them
- Realizing that you are an addict who is recovering gradually hence the need to not fall back to the bad eating habits

Treatment of Eating Disorder or Food Addiction

Treating this kind of addiction need to focus on the psychological, emotional, and physical needs of the person affected. Treatment focuses on destroying the habit of too much consumption of food and its main goal is to replace improper eating manners with healthy and better eating habits that address the issues.

Important Truths about food addiction and emotions

- If the disorder is not treated, emotional deregulation may increase the individual relapsing after the treatment
- Lack of enough skills to regulate the addiction. The symptoms may become a way of regulation of uncomfortable and overwhelming emotions
- One of the most common triggers for food addiction is negative emotions
- Most people say that they lack the proper skills to maintain their emotion in a healthy way
- Some persons with this kind of addiction say that they have difficulties in describing, expressing, and keeping up with their emotions.

Dialectical behavior therapy strives to improve commitment through motivation. It gives more attention to increasing motivational change. Given that many persons feel ambivalent and are not sure of changing their symptoms, this is very important. It also makes the addicts to non-judgmentally accept the reality and themselves in the current circumstances with the aim of meeting the goals and change behaviors that will deter them from achieving what they are purposed for.

The therapy also strives to increase self-esteem and personal confidence. The doctor puts much emphasis on the reinforcement of positive characters and seeing their patients as strong and someone who will overcome the situation in a matter of time. In this way, the self-control and self-confidence of the patient increases and they are capable of managing their experiences and situations.

It also includes detailed skills training that is aimed at better managing the symptoms and get involved in more effective coping manners.
Here are some of the skill modules taught in this book:

- Regulating Emotions- here, people are taught on how to describe and concentrate on their emotions and how to understand the personal emotional life without self-hatred, and judgment.
- Tolerating distress – it is all about learning of new techniques of passing through a crisis without increasing problems that were already there.
- Interpersonal Effectiveness - persons with food addiction problem say that they have difficulties in accepting their needs and letting what they had purposed in life to come in the forefront.
- Being Mindful - this skill is taught and modeled on how to concentrate their attention on the present moment with no judgment. It teaches the addict how to let go of painful and distracting thoughts that most of the time is the cause of the symptoms.

Lastly, another component of dialectical behavior therapy is abstinence where the addict learns to forge ahead despite all what is being said or done. It helps the addict to develop the behavior and skill to expect potential triggers and for them to take preventive measures to avoid the temptations of the trigger so that they will not go back to their old self.

If you decide on cutting out certain foods to overcome addiction, there are a few things that you can do to make it easier to accommodate the changes:

- Fast foods restaurants: You can make a list of restaurants serving fast foods and take note of any healthy food in their menu. This may prevent you from relapsing when you are tired and not ready to cook.
- Trigger foods: You should have a list of foods you crave and binge on - they are the foods you must avoid completely.

You should consider coming up with a list of pros and cons and keep one in your kitchen, wallet, or glove apartment.
Once you have taken all the steps listed above, you can choose

a date such as on a weekend from which point you will not eat the addictive foods again.

Dialectical Behavior Therapy for Treating Food Addiction

Dialectical therapy is one of the most effective ways of treating food addiction disorders. There are various choices when deciding on which kind of therapy to use. Dialectical behavior therapy is a specific type of behavioral treatment invented in 1970 by Marsha Linehan. It was used to treat people diagnosed with chronic suicide attempts or people diagnosed with borderline personality disorder. It is currently used in treating other mental disorders such as substance dependence, eating disorders, traumatic stress disorders, and depression.

Dialectical Behavior Therapy (DBT) consists of five components that include:

I.   Personal Therapy

It focuses on making sure that clients are motivated and helps them apply the skills to challenging events in life. Personal therapy occurs once every week and runs concurrently with other DBT programs such as Skills training.

II.   Skills Training

It is conducted in a group such as in a classroom where group leaders teach and assign homework on behavioral skills. Homework helps customers practice using acquired skills in daily life. Each group meets once per week, and the full skills curriculum takes 24 weeks to finish.

III. Generalization of skills through coaching

DBT makes use of telephone coaching to provide support to its customers. The objective is to teach customers how to utilize their skills to cope with problems that happen in life. They may call their personal therapist to get further coaching at any time when they require help.

IV. Consultation Team

DBT has a consultation team that gives support to various team members who provide DBT treatment. They include case managers, training group leaders, and, personal therapists who help treat customers.

V. Case Management

Case management techniques help customers manage their life, such as their social and physical environment.

Other types of Dialectical Behavior Therapy

There are many therapists who employ DBT skills to treat customers. Some therapists provide standalone training. Nevertheless, individual elements of DBT treatment can be beneficial but not as helpful compared to receiving all the five components.

Even though cognitive behavioral therapy (CBT) is effective for patients with food addiction, it does not yield positive results for every person. This has resulted in the need for researchers to come up with alternative treatment for patients who do not respond positively to CBT.

Summary

To overcome food addiction, it is necessary for you to have a plan. You can make a list of your favorite foods and decide when you will eat instead. Besides, you can have a timetable that constantly reminds you of what to eat and at what time. Adding restrictions and hunger to your plan can only make it worse. You should not set up yourself for failure by going on a diet.

Conclusion

Addicts should learn on ways of coping with stressful situations by not letting them get distracted, devoid of self-judging. It is also important to understand the health complications that addiction causes. Some health conditions can cause a person to lose his or her life. Most effects of addiction are adverse such as alcohol and drug addiction. These are either physical or psychological adverse effects. The human body, when induced to substance abuse, rapidly adapts to operating with that level of the adjusted physiological state.

That is why it is better to detect symptoms of addiction in the early stages so as to be dealt with as early as possible. Porn addiction is fast growing among the youth and teenagers, and hence the importance to learn more about it and ways to help addicts in their early stages of the addiction. Dialectical behavior therapy can be a key solution to the addiction of porn since porn addiction is multifaceted.

Dealing with Addiction, Dialectical behavior therapy comes with a more pragmatic procedure in understanding and overcoming the various forms of addiction. The strength of Dialectical behavior therapy is anchored on the cognitive behavioral concept that is interpreted as a way of cognitive behavior therapy. It recommends inviting the participation of the addict.

In this kind of therapy, it is important that the therapy is implemented to every little detail by a knowledgeable and qualified person to improve the likelihood of its success. The success of this therapy session is brought about by the client and the therapist forming a collaborative counseling relationship hence it should be noted that the therapy should not be forced on everyone even though it is generic and can be invoked to any person grappling with various kind of addiction.

Description

Have you ever asked yourself how and why people get into the addiction of various substances and habits, such as porn and online gambling? These are just some of the addiction that some individuals get into without their knowledge.
You will realize that there is no addiction that is more serious than the other. They all have similar and greater risks to the addicts.

At first, you may think that you are just taking a substance for pleasure or doing a habit because you want to do it. But as time goes by you get used to it and finally end up not being able to control its consumption and the inability to stop using the substance.

In this book, we are going to learn more about the various forms of addiction and their:
- Effects,
- Symptoms,
- How they differ from each other, and
- Overcoming the various kinds of addiction.

In this book, we will also discuss in details the information about the specific addictions:
- Porn
- Alcohol and Drugs
- Online Gambling
- Food

How does this addiction differ in terms of their symptoms and long-term and short-term effects? Different addictions have different repercussions on different users.

We shall also discuss ways of overcoming this addiction, and in particular, we will discuss how Dialectical Behavior Therapy can be applied to help the addicts overcome addiction.

Further, we will also discuss Dialectical Behavior therapy modules for:
- Emotion regulation
- Interpersonal effectiveness
- Core mindfulness
- Distress tolerance

This will help us discuss means or ways of implementing the Dialectical behavior therapy that covers the following basic areas:
- Collaborative Approach
- Support-driven
- Cognitive behavior

By the end of reading this book, you will be able to understand the various forms of addiction and how you can detect them at early stages, as well as ways to control or prevent adverse effects of addiction. You will also be able to understand in-depth how Dialectical Behavior Therapy works, and how it is applied in treating addictions, especially in the context of online gambling, porn, food addiction, and alcohol.

Addiction is a disease that can be addressed if we all come together and fight with vigor and zeal. We should be each other's keeper; let's correct one another if the path being taken by one is the wrong path.

To our reader, this book will really enlighten you and will impart more knowledge to you on the different types of Addiction and Dialectical behavior therapy as a means to help overcome them.

Made in United States
North Haven, CT
30 June 2022

20807340R00045